You Can Make An
INSECT ZOO

by Hortense Roberta Roberts

Photographs and Cages by Francis Munger

AN ELK GROVE BOOK

 CHILDRENS PRESS, CHICAGO

To Andrew, Alan, Tracy, Judith,
and all our friends
who like to watch things grow

Library of Congress Cataloging in Publication Data

Roberts, Hortense Roberta.
  You can make an insect zoo.

  SUMMARY: Directions for making cages and caring
for butterflies, moths, crickets, lady beetles, and
ants.
  "An Elk Grove book."

  Bibliography: p.
  1. Insects as pets—Juvenile literature.
[1. Insects as pets] I. Munger, Francis, 1902–
illus. II. Title.
SF459.I5R6   638'.5   73-15917
ISBN 0-516-07628-0

You Can Make An
INSECT
ZOO

Acknowledgments

Our thanks to the Pacific Grove Chamber of Commerce for information, and to Henry Chu for letting us take his picture for this book.

Contents

1. *Swallowtail Butterfly*
2. *Cricket*
3. *Lady Beetle*
4. *Aphids*
5. *Ants*

The Insect Zoo

Have fun. Make an insect zoo.

You don't have to go to a city zoo to see strange animals. You can make your own animal zoo with insects. You can make cages for them in your own home, and even carry the cages to school to show your friends. You can go hunting and bring home insects you never noticed before.

When they're in their cages, you can watch and see how they live. Many of them grow and change so much, you wouldn't know they were the same insect if you didn't see them every day.

To make the cages in your zoo, it takes only a few things that you can find around the house or in the store for a few cents.

You will need such things as

- cardboard boxes
- clear plastic drinking glasses
- corrugated cardboard
- colored construction paper
- clear wrapping plastic
- paper towels
- white glue.

You'll be the zoo keeper, so you'll give each insect food and water when it needs it. You'll want to keep your insects healthy and comfortable.

If you follow the directions in this book, you'll discover a whole new animal world. You'll be an *entomologist* (EN-to-MOL-o-jist), a person who studies insects. Best of all, it won't cost very much money, and most of the cages are easy to make.

Butterfly and Moth Cages

Some people say butterflies are the prettiest of all insects. They're as bright-colored as flowers. From spring through fall, wherever there are trees and flowers, gardens and woods, you see them flying. If you live where it is warm most of the year, you can see butterflies all year.

But do you know what butterflies look like before they become butterflies, and how they grow? Start your insect zoo by making a butterfly cage and find out.

You can make four kinds of cages: the plastic drinking glass cage (p. 9), the cardboard box cage (p. 15), he milk carton cage (p. 14), and the wire screen cage (p. 20). Some are easier to make than others. You may already have the materials for some and not for others.

First read the list of materials and directions for all four cages. Then you can decide which ones you want to make.

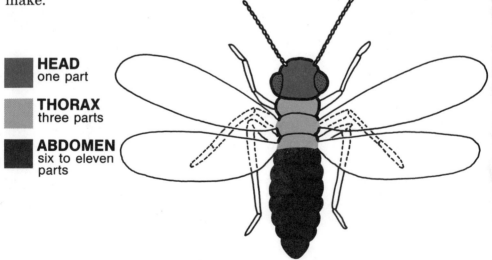

HEAD
one part

THORAX
three parts

ABDOMEN
six to eleven parts

PLASTIC
DRINKING
GLASS
CAGE

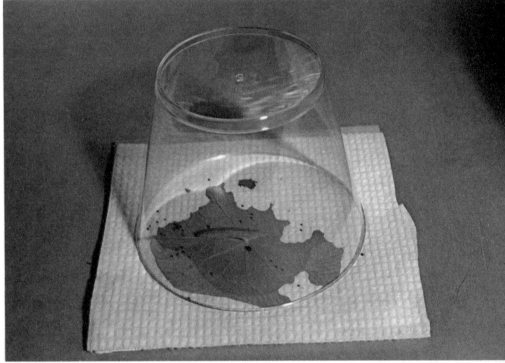

A Cabbage Butterfly caterpillar is eating a nasturtium leaf in this cage.

This cage is easiest to make. You can use it to grow two or three butterflies of the same kind, or to hatch the eggs of one kind of butterfly. You will need

    1. a clear plastic drinking glass about 3½ inches across the open end and about 2¾ inches tall (see picture) ———— You can usually buy these

glasses at a supermarket or a beverage store for a few cents. You'll need eight glasses if you make all the cages in this book.

2. a piece of corrugated cardboard 4½ inches square for the floor of the cage, which is also the feeding board for the insects—You can cut it out of a strong corrugated box from the supermarket.

3. white paper toweling cut 4½ inches square

Lay the toweling on top of the cardboard. Put the glass, open end down, on the toweling, and your cage is done. Now you're ready to grow butterflies or moths in this cage in your zoo.

All butterflies, moths, beetles, and some other kinds of insects grow in 4 stages.

1. egg 2. *larva* 3. *pupa* 4. adult

This Cabbage Butterfly came to drink nectar from mustard flowers.

Adult butterflies will not lay eggs in your cage, so you shouldn't start by catching a butterfly. Instead you should hunt for an egg, a larva, or a pupa. It's most fun to start with an egg. Then you can watch it change through all four stages in your cage. But you'll have to do some detective work. Insect eggs are no bigger than the head of a pin, and the female butterfly usually lays them on the underside of leaves.

The Cabbage Butterfly may be easiest to start in your zoo, since it lives almost everywhere in America and Europe. Its wings are white or yellowish white, about an inch long. The female has two black spots on each front wing, the male only one. The female lays her eggs on several plants including cabbage, wild mustard, and nasturtiums. *She lays them on the kind of plant the larvae will eat.*

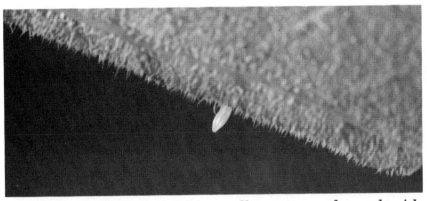

A Cabbage Butterfly laid her yellow egg on the underside of a nasturtium leaf.

Look on the leaves. The egg will be a tiny yellow dot. Put this leaf with the egg on it in your cage. If you look at the egg through a *magnifying glass,* it looks larger, like the one in the picture.

In warm weather the egg will hatch in about a week from the time it was laid. A tiny yellow, worm-like larva comes out of the egg. The butterfly larva is called a *caterpillar.*

Remember, for food, your caterpillar will need fresh leaves from the same kind of plant where you found the egg. When the leaves are wilted or the towel is dirty, throw them away and put in a clean piece of towel and fresh leaves.

A nasturtium leaf is this caterpillar's dinner.

This Cabbage Butterfly caterpillar becomes green as it eats and grows. Several times it grows too large for its skin, crawls out of it, and eats it. Then it eats more leaves and grows. Don't forget to put in fresh leaves and a clean towel every two or three days.

The caterpillar grows to be an inch long when it is about two weeks old. Then it's ready to stop eating and become a pupa. A butterfly pupa is also called a *chrysalis,* or a *chrysalid.*

After a caterpillar stops eating, it turns into a chrysalid.

If you're lucky, you can watch the caterpillar *pupate,* or change into a chrysalid. The caterpillar crawls up the side of the cage and spins a thin mat of silk. Watch it fasten its body to the cage and the mat with a belt of silk threads.

The caterpillar sheds its head-covering and skin. Then, before your eyes, it wiggles and changes its shape. It looks like the chrysalid in the picture except that it is green, and ¾ inch long.

For about two weeks the chrysalid does not move. Its outside color gradually changes from green to tan. Inside, it is changing too. You can see the shape of wings and the wing veins through the chrysalid skin. Soon, then, the skin splits open and the butterfly comes out.

At first its wings are crumpled. Slowly it pumps the juices from its body into the wing veins until the wings are large and stiffened.

For several hours the butterfly rests and should not be touched. You can look at it through a magnifying glass and see that its wings look powdery. The powder is really layers of tiny scales that would mar and rub off easily.

When the butterfly begins to flutter around the cage, take the cage outdoors. Lift the glass off the feeding board and let the butterfly go. It will fly away to drink nectar from flowers, mate, and if it is a female, lay eggs.

If you want to grow several kinds of butterflies at a time, you can make several small cages. Or you can make one of the three larger cages for all of them.

CARDBOARD BOX CAGE

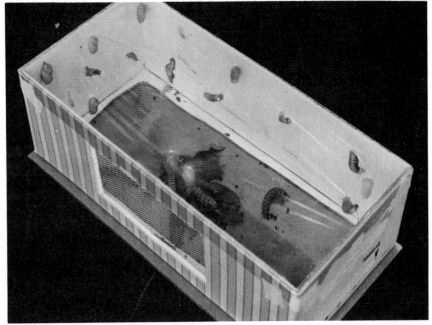

You can grow several kinds of butterflies together in this cardboard box cage.

This cage is a bottomless box set on a corrugated cardboard floor. The floor is used as a feeding board. The top is clear plastic so you can watch what happens inside the cage. There's a hole in one side of the box for a window. It's covered with netting to let in air. You will need

1. a stiff cardboard box without the lid—The one in the picture is a large shoe box. Any cardboard box about that size will do. It should be at least three inches tall. A new butterfly needs that

much space to stretch its wings. Otherwise it will be crippled and unable to fly. If the box is white inside, you can see the insects better.

2. scotch tape, or masking tape
3. a 3½ by 6 inch piece of old nylon stocking or fine netting
4. a piece of corrugated cardboard, strong and flat, about one inch longer and wider than the bottom of the box
5. white paper toweling the size of the corrugated cardboard
6. clear wrapping plastic
7. white glue, pencil, ruler

Draw a line on the box bottom, one inch from each side and end and curved at the corners. Also draw a rectangle two inches high and four inches wide in the middle of one side of the box.

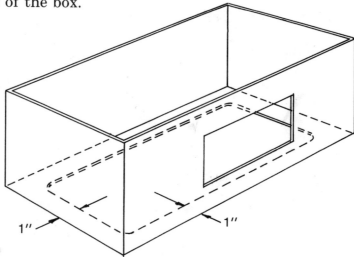

Carefully cut out the bottom of the box inside the line. Cut out the rectangle on the side. This is a little difficult. You may need help, depending on how much you have used tools.

Glue the nylon or netting inside the box to cover the window. (see diagram, p. 17)

Cover the open top of the box with a piece of clear wrapping plastic. It should be 1½ inches wider and longer than the board. Bring it down on the sides and ends, making it smooth. Fold at the corners. Fasten all around with tape.

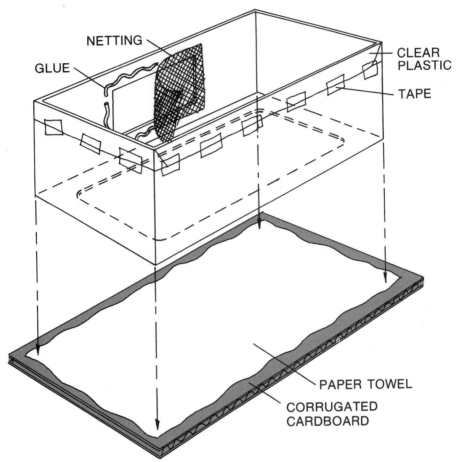

If you want to, you can glue colored paper or pictures over the printing on the box. This is your cage.

Cover the top of the corrugated feeding board with a piece of wrapping plastic 1½ inches wider and longer than the board. Smooth, fold at the corners, and fasten with tape.

Put the piece of paper towel on the feeding board. Then put the cage on the board. Your cage should look like the one in the picture on p. 15. Now, it's ready to use.

MILK
CARTON
CAGE

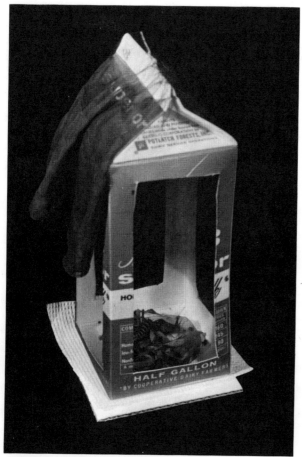

A Monarch caterpillar is eating
milkweed leaves in this cage.

This cage is a milk carton with windows cut out on four sides. There's a hole in the bottom and a cardboard feeding floor. The cage is slipped into a nylon stocking.

You will need

1. a ½ gallon milk carton
2. a fine nylon stocking
3. paper toweling and a five-inch square of corrugated cardboard for the floor and feeding board

Wash the carton. If it is smelly, put one teaspoon of baking soda into the wash water. With a pencil, mark where the windows will be on all four sides of the carton. Leave one inch all around each window for strength.

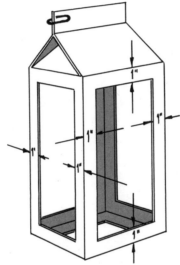

With sturdy kitchen scissors, cut the four windows. Close the top of the carton with staples or a paper clip. Cut a three inch hole in the bottom of the carton. This will let you put insects and food in the cage.

Slip the carton, bottom end first, into the nylon stocking. Let about six inches of the stocking hang over the top of the cage. (Take care not to bend the cage corners.) Cut the stocking off near the bottom, leaving about two inches to keep the stocking from slipping up over the cage.

Put caterpillars and leaves on the feeding board and set the cage down over them. When the towel gets dirty, put a fresh one on the feeding board.

WIRE
SCREEN
CAGE

*This cage is easy to make if you can
get wire screen and two plastic bleach
bottles.*

This is a cage made from two plastic bottle bottoms
and a wide tube made of window screen. You can't see
through screen as well as you can through clear plastic, or
nylon stocking. Otherwise this is a good cage. To make it

You will need

1. two 1-gallon round, plastic bottles, the kind liquid bleach comes in
2. a piece of new or used window screen nine by twenty-two inches—Maybe you can get it at a shop where they make or replace window screens.
3. five straight pins

Cut the bottom off each bottle, leaving 1½ inches of the sides. Bend the twenty-two inches of screen around to make a tube nine inches tall. Each end of the tube should be just big enough to fit into a bottle bottom. Fasten the tube together with the pins where the sides overlap.

Set the tube into a bottle bottom. Cover it with the other bottle bottom, and the cage is done.

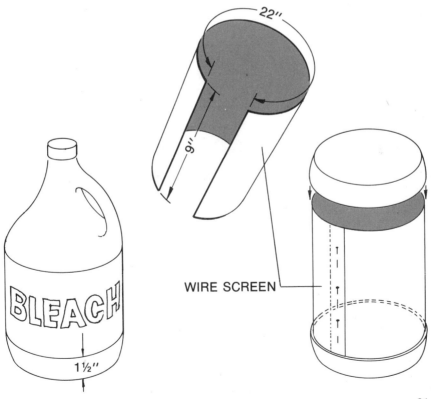

WIRE SCREEN

SOME KINDS OF BUTTERFLIES

All four cages are good for growing most kinds of butterflies. You may like to watch a *Fritillary*, a *Swallowtail*, a *Monarch*, or a *Mourning Cloak*, if they are where you live.

The Fritillary lives in places from New Jersey to Argentina. In Southern California and farther south, this caterpillar feeds on passionflower vines. Farther north some Fritillary caterpillars eat violet leaves. The eggs are gold-colored, the caterpillars very prickly black and orange.

A Fritillary came to lay eggs on a passionflower vine. If it closed its wings, you could see that the undersides look silver and gold.

A Fritillary laid this gold-colored egg on a passionflower leaf.

In the cage the Fritillary egg hatched and grew into a prickly caterpillar.

The Swallowtail was named for the tails on its hind pair of wings.

Swallowtails got their name because of the tails on their hind pair of wings. They live in many parts of the world, and there are many different kinds of Swallowtails. Among the caterpillars' favorite foods are carrot leaves, parsley, celery, and anise. Some Swallowtail caterpillars eat the leaves of trees including cottonwood, elm, popular, and wild cherry.

This young Swallowtail caterpillar is black with orange-colored spots. It will be green with black bands when it is ready to pupate.

This Monarch came to drink nectar from milkweed flowers.

The Monarch is one of the most interesting butterflies. The caterpillar is ringed with white, yellow, and black. The beautiful chrysalid is bright green with gold dots. In autumn Monarchs fly far, away from winter weather, just as birds do.

A Monarch laid her eggs on this milkweed plant.

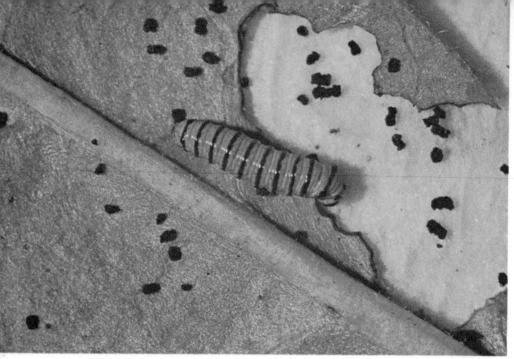

A Monarch caterpillar feeds on milkweed, the only plant that it will eat.

Entomologists in North America study how far Monarchs fly. These entomologists fasten a tiny numbered tag on the Monarch's wing and keep a copy of the number. A Mexican schoolboy found one of these tagged Monarchs. It flew from Canada to Mexico, 1,870 miles, in four months.

The children of Pacific Grove, California, have a parade and festival every autumn to celebrate when the thousands of Monarchs come to stay during the mild winter.

In the spring the Monarchs fly back to lay their eggs on milkweed, the *only* plant their larva (caterpillar) will eat. You can grow Monarchs in your cages if you live where there are milkweeds and Monarchs in spring and summer.

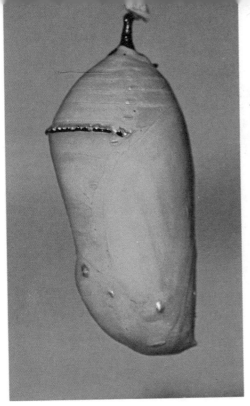

A Monarch caterpillar turns into a green chrysalid with gold spots.

When a butterfly first breaks out of the chrysalid skin, the wings are small and wrinkled.

The Mourning Cloak is one of the earliest butterflies of spring.

The Mourning Cloak is another butterfly you may like to grow. It is one of the earliest butterflies of spring. Look for the eggs and caterpillars on elm, willow, or poplar trees. The caterpillar is purplish-black and spiny with a row of red spots along the back.

Mourning Cloaks live in many places in the world including North America, Asia, and Europe. A few are found in England. The English call the Mourning Cloak the Camberwell Beauty.

Most butterflies do not live as long as Mourning Cloaks. Sometimes they find a secret, sheltered place and sleep through the winter. They may come out and fly on warm winter days.

Sometimes a Mourning Cloak will become friendly like a pet bird.

The Dog Face is the State Butterfly of California. The male has a bright-colored dog face on each front wing.

The California Dog Face butterfly, also called the Flying Pansy, is bright yellow. The male has a colorful dog face, outlined in black, on each front wing. The female is all yellow except for a dark spot on each front wing.

You may find these butterflies from California south into Mexico. Because they fly fast, they are often hard to catch. In June and July there are many of them in western California north of San Francisco.

The egg is light green. The caterpillar is green with black dots. It feeds on a bush called False Indigo. The chrysalid is bright green.

In New York, Wisconsin, Minnesota, and south to Central America, you may find other kinds of Dog Face butterflies. Some of the caterpillars eat clover and other plants.

The California Dog Face butterfly is the State Butterfly of California. Perhaps you can find out if there are other State Butterflies.

Watch for other kinds of butterflies where you live. See what plants they go to. That is where they are most likely to lay their eggs.

MOTHS

Moths and butterflies belong to an *order* called Lepi-doptera (LEP-i-DOP-ter-a), a Greek word that means scale-winged. Any insect having wings covered with scales is in the order, Lepidoptera. Moths usually fly at night, butterflies in the daytime. Moths usually have feathery feelers called *antennae* (an-TEN-ee). Butterflies have smooth antennae with a little knob at the end. Most moth caterpillars spin around themselves a silk covering called a *cocoon*. Then they pupate. Butterfly caterpillars never spin cocoons. They change into pupae called chrysalids.

Perhaps in your zoo, you will find other ways that moths and butterflies are different.

You can grow some kinds of moths in cages. The larvae of others crawl underground or under the bark of trees to pupate. Some moths, like the Luna and Hawkmoth, are too large for your cages.

In the library you can find books with colored pictures of butterflies and moths. These books tell the names of those that live near you. They also tell on what kind of plant or tree to look for eggs and caterpillars. See the book list on p.

Be careful when you bring an egg, caterpillar, chrysalid, or cocoon in from outdoors. Carry it on the leaf or stem where you found it; and don't drop it, squeeze it, or tear the chrysalid from its silk mat. Tape the leaf or stem on or near the top of the cage. The chrysalid or cocoon must hang just the way you found it.

Sometimes you'll find an egg, larva, or pupa and not know what it is. Put it in a cage by itself, because some insects eat other insects. When it's a larva, bring fresh food of the kind it was on when you found it. Then watch and see what happens.

The Cricket Cage

Everyone has heard the "Chirr—Chirr" of crickets outdoors at night. Maybe you've heard it in the house. It probably was a cricket. You can have one or more crickets in your zoo if you are smart enough to find and catch them.

The cricket is a little black or brown insect. Like most insects, it has three parts to its body, three pairs of legs, and two long antennae. Because it has long hind legs, it can jump fast and scurry away.

Crickets like to crawl into the paper hideaways at the back of their cage to get away from light.

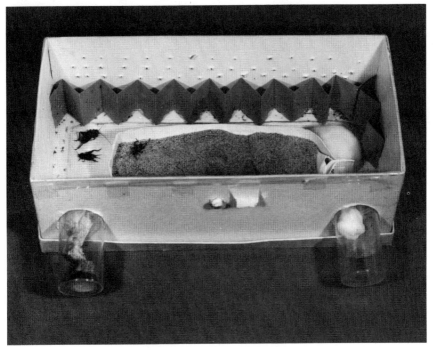

This cage is a bottomless box. The box lid is kept under it for a floor that can be removed for cleaning. Two plastic vials in holes on the front will hold food and water. There is a tray of sand or earth where the crickets can dig, and females can lay their eggs. Across the back wall inside the cage is a row of construction paper hideaways where crickets like to rest or crawl in and out.

To make the cage you will need

1. a stiff cardboard box with the lid — The one in the picture is a big shoe box.
2. white paper toweling the size of the inside of the box lid
3. bright-colored construction paper
4. clear wrapping plastic
5. scotch tape or masking tape
6. two round clear-plastic vials about 1½ inches across and 2½ inches tall, the kind pills come in
7. an empty 1-quart milk carton
8. about two cups of sand or garden earth
9. a piece of corrugated cardboard just big enough to cover the top of the box
10. several cotton balls, or some cotton
11. a four-inch glass eyedropper with straight tip
12. white glue, pencil, ruler

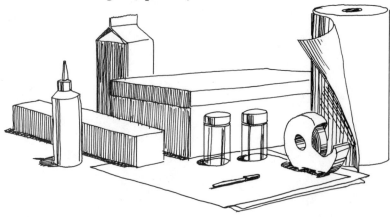

Put the lid on the bottom of the box. On the front of the box, draw two circles just above the box lid and about one inch from each end of the box. To draw circles, hold the bottom of one of the vials against the box, and draw around it. Cut out circles. Holes should be just large enough for vials to fit snugly. (See picture, page 31.)

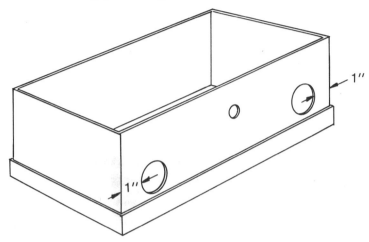

Remove box lid. Cut a ½ inch round hole in the middle of the front of the box about 1½ inches from the top. Plug it with a small piece of cotton.

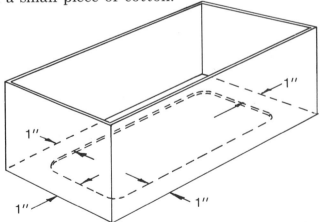

Draw a line on the box bottom, one inch from each side and end, and curved at corners. Cut out the bottom inside the line.

33

To make the hideaways, cut a strip of contruction paper two inches wide and twenty-four inches long. Draw lines one inch apart across the strip. Then fold it back and forth on the lines as if you were going to make a fan.

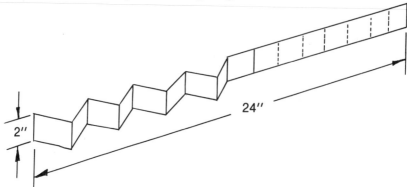

2"

24"

Put glue on the back and part of one end of the cage, inside, near the bottom. Press the folds on one side of the paper against the glue, about one inch apart. The folds should stick out about ⅞ of an inch. Now you have places for the crickets to hide.

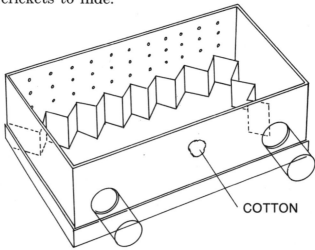

COTTON

Above the hideaways make three rows of small holes about one inch apart in the wall, for air. You can make the holes with a small nail or the sharp end of a drawing compass.

Glue a cotton ball inside the cage under each vial hole. The cotton helps the crickets to climb into the vials.

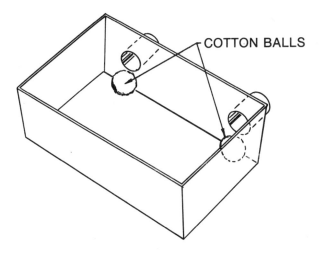

COTTON BALLS

Cover the top of the box with a piece of wrapping plastic 1½ inches wider and longer than the box. Bring the plastic down on the sides and ends, making it smooth. Fold at the corners. Fasten with tape. This is your cage.

Put the box cover, top side down, on the table and lay the piece of paper towel on it. This is the floor of the cage.

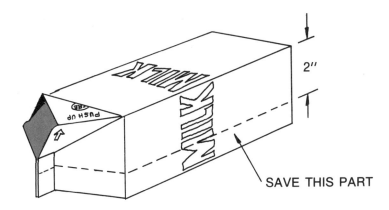

2"

SAVE THIS PART

Cut off and throw away two inches from the opened side of the 1-quart milk carton. Fill the tray with earth, almost to the top. This is where the crickets can dig, and the females lay their eggs. Set the tray in the middle of the cage floor and put the cage on top. Glue a ball of cotton to the outer side of the tray near the pointed end so the crickets can crawl into it easily.

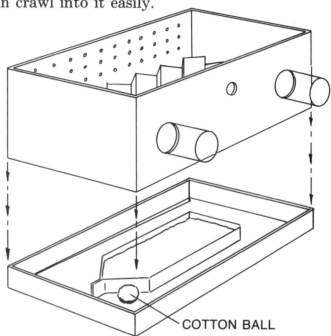

COTTON BALL

To catch a cricket you'll need a glass jar and a piece of thin cardboard, maybe a postcard, large enough to cover the opening of the jar.

Most any time of year, you may find a cricket in your house. Outdoors, it's easiest to find a cricket on a warm summer evening. The warmer the weather, the oftener and faster a cricket sings. If you hear one, take your jar, cardboard, and a flashlight.

The cricket will suddenly stop singing when you come near it. Stand still. Be quiet till it sings again. Turn your flashlight on it. Be very quick before it jumps. Put the jar down over it and slide the cardboard under it.

Before you put the cricket in your cage, be sure the sand or earth in the carton is damp but not muddy.

Put bits of food in one of the vials. Crickets eat small pieces of apple or melon, raw squash, whole-wheat bread, cooked chicken or meat, and freshly-killed insects, especially flies. Like people, crickets need a balanced diet of bread, vegetables, fruit, and meat. If they don't have enough food, they may chew their way out through the walls of the cage, or even eat each other.

Put the food vial into one of the cage holes. Cotton wet with drinking water goes in the other vial, but don't put it in yet.

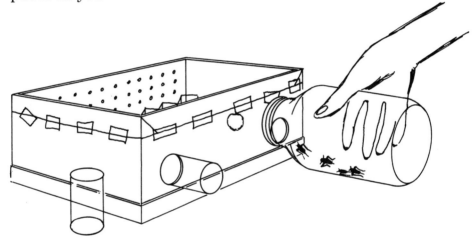

Hold the jar with the cricket in it over the open hole. Slide the cardboard out between the jar and the hole. Wait till the cricket goes into the cage. Then put the water vial in its hole.

Crickets like to be in the shade, so you should cover the cage with the piece of corrugated cardboard. Take the cover off when you want to watch the crickets.

Keep the vials clean. Throw away the wilted food and the wet cotton when it gets dirty. Put in fresh food and wet cotton whenever it's needed.

Later, the earth may dry out. Wet it with the dropper through the small hole in the front of the cage. Don't forget to put cotton in the hole again.

The cricket on the left is a male. You can tell by the raised, curved lines on its wings.

When the cage needs cleaning, watch until none of the crickets are on the cage floor or the earth tray. Then quickly lift the cage from its floor and set it on a table. Don't spill the earth. There might be eggs in it. Throw away the dirty paper towel and put in a clean one. Set the cage back on its floor when your crickets are away from the bottom opening.

It's fun to find the crickets yourself. If you can't, perhaps you can buy a few from an aquarium store or a fish bait store.

Don't try to keep more than five or six crickets in the cage together because the males may fight each other. Have one or two females if you can. The female's wings are smooth. The male has raised, curved lines on his wings.

A cricket is never a larva or pupa like a butterfly or moth. The female lays her eggs in the earth. Tiny crickets without wings hatch from the eggs. A baby cricket is called a *nymph*. It grows and changes its skin eight times. The last time, it becomes an adult with wings that lie straight along its back.

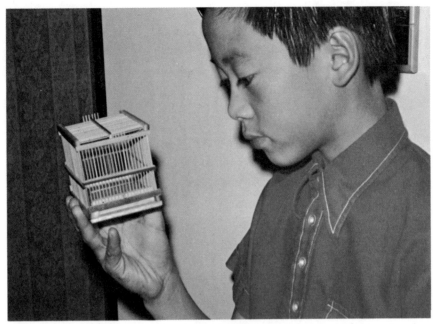

The male cricket is the one that sings. In Japan and China people keep them in cages for pets.

In warm weather cricket eggs hatch in fifteen days and the nymphs become adults in eight weeks. When the female lays her eggs outdoors in fall, they usually hatch the next spring. They may hatch in winter where the weather is warm.

Adult crickets have two pairs of wings, one on top of the other. The male cricket makes his song by rubbing his top wings together. The female cricket cannot sing, but she can listen. Like the male, she has ears in her knees.

In Japan and China people keep male crickets in pretty little cages for pets. They love to hear the crickets' song.

Crickets belong to an order called Orthoptera (Or-THOP-ter-a). Many insects with straight wings are in the order, Orthoptera.

Lady Beetle Cage

Most people like lady beetles. They help gardeners and farmers. They eat billions of tiny insects that suck the juices from flowers, fruit, and vegetables.

Lady beetles eat tiny insects that kill plants.

A lady beetle is only about ¼ inch long. It is shaped like half a ball. The two shiny hard wings on top are usually dark red, orange, or yellow. Sometimes they have black spots.

The cage is easy to make. It's the same as the small butterfly cage on page 9. If you want to grow lady beetles from eggs, make two cages, one for the beetles and one for eggs.

The best time to find lady beetles is spring and summer. The best place to find them is where they are eating. Tiny, soft-bodied insects called *aphids* (A-fids) are one of their favorite foods. Pages 45-47 tell you more about aphids and where to find them.

To catch lady beetles, take a glass jar, a piece of cloth big enough to cover the opening, and a rubber band. Find a plant with a lady beetle on it.

The lady beetle looks slow and easy to catch, but it isn't. Before you know it, it can lift its hard wings and unfold its two thin wings from underneath. The thin wings move so fast, the lady beetle almost disappears when it flies.

Hold the jar as close as you can under a beetle that's feeding. Tap the plant. If you are lucky, the beetle will fall into the jar. Be quick. Cover the opening with the cloth and fasten it with the rubber band. Try to catch several lady beetles.

Cut some leaves or stems with aphids on them, and be careful not to shake the aphids off. Put the leaves and aphids on the feeding board of the cage, with the glass over them.

Set your jar of beetles in the refrigerator or other cool place for an hour to quiet them. Then put them in the cage under the plastic drinking glass. Work fast so they won't fly away. Now your lady beetle cage is part of the zoo and ready to watch.

Don't be surprised if a lady beetle lays eggs in the cage. The eggs are bright orange, no bigger than the head of a pin. They may be on the glass, the leaves, anywhere in the cage. If you leave them there, the lady beetles will eat them.

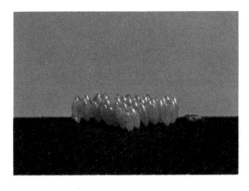

A lady beetle laid some eggs in the cage.

You can save the eggs if you keep them in one cage and the beetles in another. Be careful not to touch or crush the eggs, or let any beetles fly away.

All beetles, like butterflies, grow in four stages.

1. egg 2. larva 3. pupa 4. adult

If you get eggs from your beetles, you can watch all the changes. The eggs turn black and hatch in three to five days after they are laid. A dark, spidery little larva comes out of each egg.

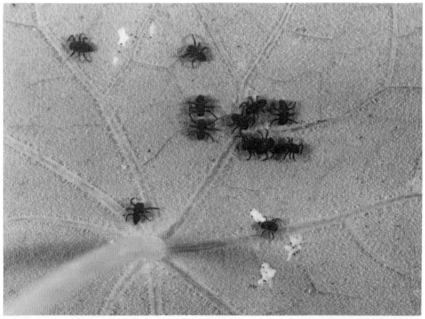

These spidery lady beetle larvae just hatched from eggs. By next day they will eat aphids on the nasturtium leaf.

At first the larvae huddle together. Next day they begin to crawl around. Put in aphids and watch the larvae eat. For several days they eat, grow, and change. Then they look like black and orange lizards or dragons, about the size of lady beetles.

*This older lady beetle larva
looks like a dragon. It
caught an aphid to eat.*

When they are ready to become *pupae,* they fasten
themselves by their tails to a leaf, stem, or the glass, and
bend double. Do not unfasten them or they will die.

For several days they won't move or eat. But you can
see that they will change both inside and out.

At last the pupa skin breaks open. A lady beetle comes
out. It looks like the lady beetle that laid the eggs. It rests
for a day, as the new larva did. Then it eats aphids. If it's
a female, it will lay eggs.

If the glass gets dirty, put a clean glass on the board.
When the beetles have eaten the aphids, take out the old
leaves and stems. Put in new ones with aphids on them.
Don't lift the glass higher than you need to. A pair of
tweezers works better than fingers for changing the leaves
and stems.

*Some lady beetles have
spots, and some do not.*

When you can't find more aphids, or when you are finished with the beetles, free them outdoors to find insects to eat.

Two kinds of lady beetles eat beans and squashes instead of insects. But most kinds of lady beetles are helpful. Farms and gardens need them.

There are people who have special houses for growing lady beetles. Farmers buy many thousands of them to eat insects that eat their crops. The beetles take the place of insecticides, or insect poisons, that might hurt people or pets and livestock.

Some people call a lady beetle a ladybird, but it's not a bird. Others call it a ladybug, but is it not a real bug. An entomologist would tell you that a bug belongs to a different order of insect.

Beetles belong to an order called Coleoptera (Ko-lee-OP-ter-a). Most insects with hard wing-covers over their flying wings are in the order, Coleoptera.

Other books tell you about many other kinds of beetles.

These are a few:

- carpet beetles that eat holes in wool rugs and cloth
- clickbeetles that fall on their backs and turn over with a clicking sound
- whirligig beetles that dart in curves on quiet water
- fireflies that glow as they fly at night
- scarabs, some of them shining red, green, and gold.

One kind of scarab has lived in Egypt for thousands of years. In museums you may see them carved out of clay or jewels. Egyptians wore them and thought they brought good luck.

Aphids

You don't need a separate cage for aphids. You'll put them in the cage to be food for your lady beetles.

The aphid is a tiny, pear-shaped insect. Most full-grown aphids are not much bigger than the head of a pin. Different kinds of aphids come in different colors: green, yellow, brown, gray, black, even red. All of them have soft bodies, easy to crush.

Aphids stick their beaks into plants and suck the juices.

Aphids are garden pests. They stick their sharp beaks into stems, new leaves, buds, and flowers, and suck their juices.

In spring and summer, aphids are born alive. One aphid can produce several baby aphids each day. Soon there are so many sucking one plant that they spoil the plant.

Most aphids are wingless. However, if the plant becomes crowded, some of the aphids grow wings, and fly to other plants to start new families.

The aphids' bodies produce a sweet syrup called *honeydew*. Ants carry aphids to plants near their ant holes. The honeydew is food for the ants. That's why the aphid is called the ants' cow. And that is why you often find ants where there are aphids.

Some plants where you are most likely to find aphids to feed your lady beetles are nasturtiums, rose bushes, apple leaves, sweet peas, peas, lettuce, cabbages, cucumbers, and weeds.

Another small sucking insect is called a mealybug, because it looks as if it were covered with white flour. You may find it on outdoor plants or on oranges and lemons. Lady beetles eat mealybugs, but you won't want to bring any indoors. They get on house plants and are hard to get rid of. Even lady beetles can't eat all of them.

A mealybug is not a real bug. Aphids and mealybugs belong to an order called *Homoptera* (Ho-MOP-ter-a). Most Homoptera have clear wings, and all have sucking mouth parts. Each wing is the same thickness all over.

PROJECTS

You can plant a nasturtium in a pot and grow aphids to feed your lady beetles.

1. Grow a nasturtium in a pot. Put one aphid from an outdoor plant on it. Use a small paint brush to move the aphid from the leaf to your plant. Keep it near your house or in a sunny window indoors. Don't forget to water it. See how many aphids there are by the next day and next week. On rainy days, or when you can't find food for your lady beetles, you can give them aphids from your nasturtiums.
2. Find the word "bug" in other insect books. What order of insect does it belong to? How does it differ from other insects? What are the names of some real bugs? Can you find any of them outdoors?

Ant Cages

We all see ants when we don't want them. Sometimes we find them at picnics, or even in the house on our cake and candy. We see long trails of ants in the garden. Sometimes an ant carries a dead fly bigger than itself. All these are worker ants. They collect food for their family underground.

Ants are more like people than almost any other insect. They take care of their young, and they feed and help each other.

You can make two kinds of cages, an eyedropper cage or a tunnel cage. One is a plastic vial with an eyedropper sticking out of the cap. The female, called the *queen,* lays eggs in the dropper. You can watch the workers feed her and the larvae in the dropper.

The other cage is harder to make. It is made so that there is sand packed between two nesting, plastic glasses. The glasses are set down in a sort of round box.

This cage lets you watch the ants as if they were living underground. You can see them dig tunnels and rooms in the sand to live in. They carry food from little plastic "dishes" above to their family below.

◀ *Ants make tunnels in this cage.*

EYEDROPPER CAGE

You will need

1. a clear plastic pill vial 1½ inches across and at least 2½ inches tall, with cap
2. a 4-inch glass eyedropper with a straight tip
3. some cotton
4. tweezers
5. a swab stick or other thin stick longer than the dropper
6. a piece of construction paper 2 inches square

The worker ants feed their queen and take care of the eggs and larvae in the eyedropper.

Near the edge of the vial cap, make a hole about ½ inch across. This hole is for air and to feed the ants. Fill the hole with cotton.

Take the rubber bulb off the glass tube of the eyedropper. Near the opposite edge of the vial cap, make a hole for the large end of the glass tube. The tube should fit tightly in the hole.

With the swab stick, pack ½ inch of cotton into the small end of the dropper. From the inner side of the vial cap, push the dropper into the small hole, way to the end. (See picture p. 50.)

Put about twelve drops of water into the rubber bulb and stick it onto the small end of the dropper. Squeeze the bulb enough to soak the cotton. Keep it wet. This is the ants' drinking fountain. It also keeps the air damp for the ants.

When you have collected the ants, put a tiny drop of honey in the vial. Brush the ants into the vial and quickly put the cap on.

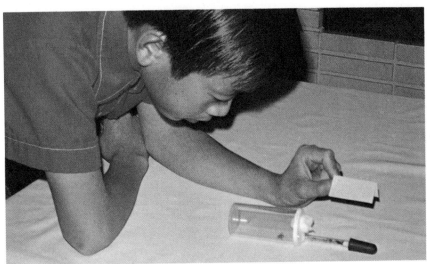

You lift the paper cover to watch the queen, but she likes to be in the dark.

Fold the piece of construction paper down the middle. Lay it over the dropper to keep the ants dark. Soon they will find the dropper and go into it. To feed them, take the cotton out of the large hole in the cap and drop in a freshly-killed fly or other food.

TUNNEL
CAGE

In this cage you can watch the ants make tunnels the way they do underground.

To make this cage you will need

1. a piece of corrugated cardboard about 8 inches square. This is the floor of the cage.
2. two clear plastic drinking glasses
3. about a cupful of fine, clean sand, the kind you find at the lake or ocean
4. the bottom 3 inches of a one half gallon milk carton—This is the cage holder and keeps the tunnels dark.

5. a piece of thin cardboard 1½ inches wide and 20 inches long—This will be glued into a ring for cage walls.
6. two plastic caps from pill vials—These are food and water "dishes."
7. a piece of clear wrapping plastic to cover the top of the cage
8. a rubber band to hold the cover on
9. cotton
10. a 4-inch glass eyedropper with a straight tip
11. tweezers

In the middle of the cage floor, make a hole. It must be a little smaller than the top of the drinking glass. To do this, put a glass upside down on the cardboard. Draw around it. Cut a smooth hole inside the line and glue the glass into it.

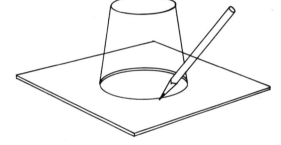

When the glue is dry, put more glue around the glass. If there are spaces between the glass and the cage floor, the ants will get away.

Put some sand in the glued glass. Set the other glass on top of the sand in the glued glass. The rim of the inside glass should stand up ½ inch higher than the other one. Wet the sand with the dropper.

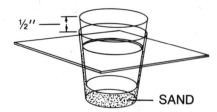

Weight the glass down with a round stone or something heavy. Fill the space between the glasses ⅔ full all around with sand. Pour three dropperfuls of water around on the sand. Then take the weight from the glass.

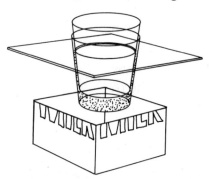

Cut the bottom three inches off the ½-gallon milk carton. This is your cage holder.

Make two holes in the middle of the 20-inch piece of cardboard. The holes should be about ½ inch wide and three inches apart. Bend and shape the cardboard to form a ring. Glue the ends together, overlapping two inches.

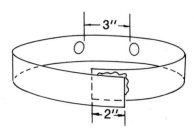

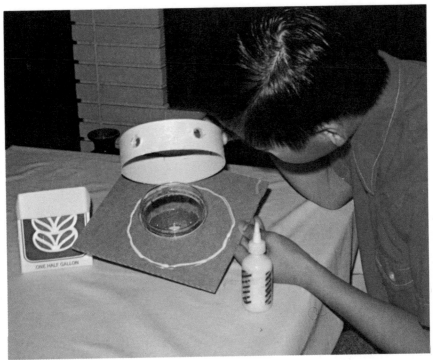

The walls of the cage are a cardboard ring. Glue it to the cage floor.

Glue the cardboard ring to the cage floor, off-center, near one corner. To do this, first spread a circle of white glue the size of the ring on the cage floor. Set the ring on

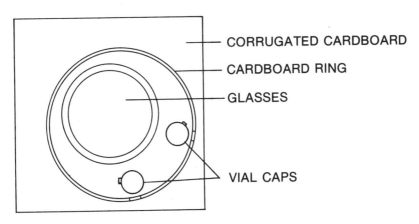

CORRUGATED CARDBOARD

CARDBOARD RING

GLASSES

VIAL CAPS

the circle of glue. Then put the cage, with the glass downward, on the open top of the cage holder. Put a heavy book on top of the ring while it is drying.

Fill the ½-inch holes with cotton and take it out only when you are giving the ants food or water. Glue the vial cap dishes to the floor inside the ring, one near each hole.

Now you are ready to put some ants in your cage and watch them. You'll want little black ants. Red ants sometimes sting people.

To hunt for an ant trail, look near the garbage can outdoors. Look near flowers and plants that have aphids. Look near walls or on the trunks of trees. When you find ants, follow their trail to the little hole in the ground where they go in and out.

To start your ant family, you'll need about thirty workers and a queen. You'll know her because she is twice the size of a worker. You could catch the workers easily, but the queen lives underground in the dark. You'll have to lure her out.

Here is one way to lure a queen. Get an empty milk carton. Put fresh bits of food in it. Ants like cake, meat, fruit, banana peelings, bacon, and a little sugar or syrup.

*In the tunnel the worker ants feed the queens and larvae
and take care of the eggs. The queens are twice the size
of the workers.*

Put the carton on a box on the ant trail near the ant hole
and go away.

Come back after several hours or the next day. Bring
a glass jar and a lid, and a soft paint brush. By then the
ants should be trailing in and out of the carton. Watch and
be patient. A queen may not come for a long time.

When you see a queen on the carton or box, brush her
quickly into the jar. Brush workers into the jar with her
and put on the lid.

If you do not find a queen, pour some water around,
not in, the ant hole. If worker ants carry white pupae out
of the hole, a queen may come soon. If she doesn't, you'll
have to dig into the nest with a spoon and trowel. Dig
carefully. Follow the hole down to the nest. When you come
to the ant family, scoop the queen with other ants into your
jar and cover it. Don't lose the queen. The workers will
not live long without her.

If you have made the tunnel cage, put a tiny drop of honey in one vial cap dish and a little wet cotton in the other. Brush the ants from the jar onto the floor of the cage. Quickly cover the cage top with the wrapping plastic. Fasten the plastic with the rubber band above the holes.

Use the dropper to keep the cotton in the dish wet. Use the tweezers to put a freshly-killed fly in the food dish. Take out the old flies. See if the ants will carry away tiny crumbs of corn flakes or cake. You can lift the cage out of the holder to watch the tunnels. Then put the cage back to keep the tunnels dark.

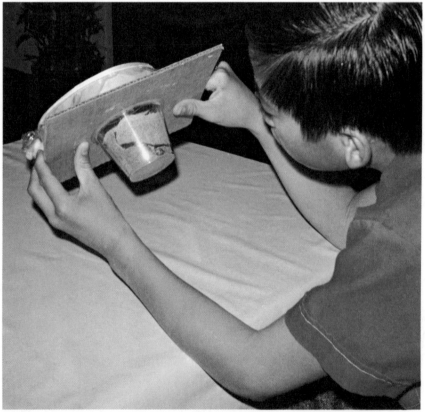

You can lift the cage out of its holder and watch the ants in the tunnels.

58

With the dropper, add a few drops of water to the sand every few days. If it's too dry, the tunnels will cave in. If it's too wet, the ants will run out. You would too, if your house filled with water.

Both the eyedropper cage and the tunnel cage should be kept where it is light and warm, but not in the sun.

You'll be surprised how many things there are to watch. The workers feed the queen mouth to mouth. The tiny eggs hatch and change from larvae to pupae to ants.

Ants belong to an order called *Hymenoptera* (HI-men-OP-ter-a), a Greek word meaning skin-winged. The wings are thin and soft like skin. Many insects, including bees and wasps, that have four skin-like wings are in the order, Hymenoptera.

When they live in the ground outdoors, male and female ants grow wings. The males and females fly and mate. Afterwards the males die. The females bite off their own wings and crawl into the earth. There they lay eggs and start new families. The workers never have wings.

If you take good care of your ants, they should live for many months, maybe years. Best of all, you can watch yours as if you were really underground.

A Notebook

You may want to keep a notebook about the insects in your zoo. You can write down

- the name of the insect
- order of insect
- where you found it
- date found
- on what kind of plant
- if it was an egg, nymph or larva, pupa, or adult
- description—color, shape, size
- how long it took the eggs to hatch
- how long it took to change from egg to larva to pupa to adult
- or how long it took to change from egg to nymph to adult
- dates when it changed its form
- how it looked before and after
- how it looked while changing
- any other interesting or unusual facts.

Entomologists keep careful notes about the insects they watch and study. That is the way they make discoveries.

There are many more insects than there are people in the world, and much to be learned about them. If you watch and think, you may learn things that nobody ever knew before.

# Word List

ORDERS OF INSECTS IN THIS BOOK

Coleoptera (CO-lee-OP-ter-a)	covered-winged	lady beetles
Homoptera (Ho-MOP-ter-a)	alike-winged	aphids mealybugs
Hymenoptera (HI-men-OP-ter-a)	skin-winged	ants
Lepidoptera (Lep-i-DOP-ter-a)	scale-winged	butterflies and moths
Orthoptera (Or-THOP-ter-a)	straight-winged	crickets

Book List

Comstock, John Henry. *An Introduction to Entomology.* Ithaca, New York: The Comstock Publishing Co., 1925.

Fabre, J. H. *Fabre's Book of Insects.* New York: Dodd, Mead.

Fanning, Eleanor Ivanye. *Insects from Close Up.* New York: Thomas Y. Crowell Company, 1965.

Jaques, H. E. *How to Know the Insects.* Dubuque: William C. Brown, Co., 1947.

Klotz, Alexander B. *A Field Guide to the Butterflies.* Boston: Houghton Mifflin, 1951.

Podendorf, Illa. *The True Book of Insects.* Chicago: Childrens Press, 1954.

Politi, Leo. *The Butterflies Come.* New York: Charles Scribner's Sons, 1957.

Roberts, Hortense Roberta. *Insects Indoors and Out.* Chicago: Melmont Publishers, Inc., 1957.

Teal, Edwin Way. *The Junior Book of Insects.* New York: E. P. Dutton & Company, Inc., 1953.

Tilden, J. W. *Butterflies of the San Francisco Bay Region.* Berkeley and Los Angeles: University of California Press, 1965.

About the Author and Photographer

Hortense Roberta Roberts is Mrs. Francis Munger in private life. Her poems, articles, and stories have appeared in more than 150 different books and periodicals including: *Atlantic, Saturday Review, Elementary English, Instructor, McCalls, Ladies' Home Journal, Parents' Magazine, American Childhood, Yankee, Westways, Chatelaine* (Canada), and *Jack and Jill,* as well as *The Christian Science Monitor, The New York Times, Prairie Schooner,* and *Poet Lore.* She is author of the book, INSECTS INDOORS AND OUT, with photographs by Mr. Munger.

Francis Munger was an entomologist with the United States Department of Agriculture for thirty years. He is Research Consultant with Whittier College, and Research Associate with the University of Toronto for which he tagged Monarchs and studied their wintering places from Laguna Beach to Pacific Grove. He conducts workshops for teachers on how to grow butterflies and silkworms, reel silk, and make papyrus. His articles, illustrated with his own drawings and photographs, have appeared in the *Journal of Research on the Lepidoptera, Journal of Economic Entomology, Science,* and various government publications.

Both author and illustrator were born in Minnesota. Both are graduates of the University of Minnesota. They have lived in Maryland and Georgia as well as in Minnesota. The Mungers now make their home in Whittier, California.

64

638   Roberts, Hortense
ROB   Roberta

       You can make an
       insect zoo

Sara 6th	DATE DUE		
	MAR 22 '01		